This book belongs to:

_____

THE POO FAIRY

Hailey McQuilken, PT, DPT

Illustrations By Amina Yaqoob

<u>Reader's Guide:</u>

Fill in the blank with your child's name for a personal touch. Encourage your little one to gain independence in the bathroom with the provided "hidden physical therapy (PT) message" for an added clinical perspective.

Meet ____!

She is a big girl who can do lots
of fun things.

_____ can climb and jump at the playground, run, and even kick a ball.

PT message: The listed activities are developmentally appropriate milestones for two years of age. They can help strengthen the core and pelvic floor. Strength is needed to have a bowel movement, but also to get on and off the toilet, maintain balance while dressing and undressing, and perform weight shifts to wipe.

Because _____ is a big girl, it's time for her to say bye-bye to diapers. It's time to poo on her potty.

PT message: Help your child understand his or her physiological cues promptly. Rushing can lead to more accidents.

Hmmm. What is that feeling in her tummy? It means she must go to the bathroom and sit on her potty.

_____ pulls down her big girl pants, sits on her potty, and sings her favorite song.

PT message: To ease evacuation, your child should be positioned on a toddler-sized toilet in a squatting position with his or her knees closer to the chest. Encourage singing while having a bowel movement to prevent unwanted breath holding.

PLOP! _____ made a poo in her potty.

Now, it's time to wipe her bottom, pull up her pants, and wash her hands. All clean!

PT message: Routines help build habits and aid in learning new skills.

The Poo Fairy will visit tonight when she is fast asleep.

Wake up! It's morning time.
____ runs to check the bathroom.

The Poo Fairy came! She left a present hidden in the bathroom. Thank you, Poo Fairy!

_____ can't wait to use her potty again and have another visit from the Poo Fairy.

PT message: Positive reinforcement goes a long way.
Avoid punishing your child for accidents.

Made in the USA
Middletown, DE
05 September 2024